Only Bread, Only Light

Only Bread,
Only Light

Poems by

Stephen Kuusisto

诗 COPPER CANYON PRESS

Grateful acknowledgment is made to the Detroit Institute of Arts for the use of *Still Life with Fallen Candles,* by Max Beckman, on the cover.

Copper Canyon Press is in residence under the auspices of the Centrum Foundation at Fort Worden State Park in Port Townsend, Washington. Centrum sponsors artist residencies, education workshops for Washington State students and teachers, blues, jazz, and fiddle tunes festivals, classical music performances, and The Port Townsend Writers' Conference.

LIBRARY OF CONGRESS CATALOGING-IN-PUBLICATION DATA

Kuusisto, Stephen.
Only bread, only light: poems / by Stephen Kuusisto.
    p. cm.
ISBN 1-55659-150-0
1. Visually handicapped — Poetry. I. Title.
PS3561.U85 O55 2000
811'.6— DC21   00-010241
CIP

9 8 7 6 5 4 3 2
FIRST PRINTING

COPPER CANYON PRESS
Post Office Box 271
Port Townsend, Washington 98368
www.coppercanyonpress.org

Grateful acknowledgment is made to the editors of publications in which the following poems, some in earlier versions, first appeared:

Books from Finland: *Drink*

Indiana Review: *Tenth Muse*

Mississippi Review: *At the Summer House*

Poetry: *Summer at North Farm*

Poetry East: *Seven Prayers*

Quarry West: *Blind Days in Early Youth, Section Two and Section Three; Competing Interests within the Family: 1909*

Seneca Review: *Blind Days in Early Youth, Section One; Breton-esque; Lying Still; Still; "Talking Books"*

Learning Braille at Thirty-Nine and *"Talking Books"* appeared originally in the anthology *Staring Back: The Disability Experience from the Inside Out*, published by Dutton.

I wish to thank the Blue Mountain Center for the Arts and the MacDowell Colony for residencies during which some of these poems were completed.

For Connie, Tara, and Ross

No one perhaps could understand
who has not been as lost as I was,
nor as far from others as I felt,
a heap of coal in the night.

Then, only bread, only light.

PABLO NERUDA
translated by Alastair Reid

Contents

Three

Only Bread, Only Light

One

Blind Days in Early Youth

No Name for It

Start with a hyphenated word, something Swedish —
Rus-blind; "blind drunk"; *blinda-fläcken;* "blind spot";

Blind-pipa; "nonentity," "a type of ghost."
En blind höna hittar också ett korn;

"The fool's arrow sometimes hits the mark."
(That's what the Swedish matron said

When I was a boy climbing stairs.)
She pointed with a cane: *Tsk tsk,*

Barna-blind; "blind child."
Her tone mixed piety and reproof — pure Strindberg!

It echoed on the stairs, *barna-blind* —
"Blind from birth." *En blind höna hittar...*

The blind child's arrow...

Terra Incognita

When I walked in the yard
Before sunrise,
I made my way among patches of dew —
Those constellations on the darkened grass.

The webs drifted like anemones,
And I thought of lifting them
As if they were skeins of brilliant yarn
That I could give to my mother
Who'd keep them
Until we knew what to make.

I pictured a shirt —
How I'd pull it over my head
And vanish in the sudden light.

Awake All Night

The cabinet radio glowed
With its lighted dial

As I pressed my face to the glass.
My spectacles, thick as dishes,

Were kaleidoscopes of light,
So I'd lean close

To make out numbers,
And the brilliant city of tubes

Just visible through a crevice.
I never heard the music

As I traced those lamp-lit houses
Like a sleepy, mindful ghost

Who looks down out of habit
At the vivid world.

Learning Braille at Thirty-Nine

The dry universe
Gives up its fruit,

Black seeds are raining,
Pascal dreams of a wristwatch,

And heaven help me
The metempsychosis of book

Is upon me. I hunch over it,
The boy in the asylum

Whose fingers leapt for words.
(In the dark books are living things,

Quiescent as cats.)
Each time we lift them

We feel again
The ache of amazement

Under summer stars.
It's a dread thing

To be lonely
Without reason.

My window stays open
And I study late

As quick, musical laughter
Rises from the street

And I rub grains of the moon
In my hands.

Accomplice

It was in the nature of things
That I couldn't see. The nature of things
That the magpie should watch me.

Perpetual strangers
Touch my sleeves,
The steel light of August

Draws me, affirming
Over brilliant and terrible streets,
And the bird looks on —

You'd swear
He's like those wounded gentlemen
From the First World War,

Watchful, innocent,
Hoarding his words
In case someone is lost.

Guess

Because waking, the radio low,
I've heard music by unnamed composers,
The puzzle of melody returns me
To the viola, *Kol Nidrei,*
Or the oldest songs of the Finns.

The fields are swept by a music
Half-heard when rising,
No sound, blue intervals,
Then the next phrase
While rain streaks the windows
And the vibrato of recurrent wind
Tells of the waning moon
And Mendelssohn's fiddle.

It's a private, chalked-out game
As December collects and snow begins.
All morning I carry other people's words,
Advance the clock, talk through habit,
But early, the music lets me stand —
Freed from opinion into guess,
A place I need as some need ends.
I walk between pillars of silk,
Hear the rhapsody of Solomon.
The Hebraic dawn opens again,
A windfall, and I hesitate.

Dante's *Paradiso* Read Poorly in Braille

Each morning
I live with less color:
The lawn turns gray,
The great laurel is gravid
With flint — as if it might burn
In the next life.
Even the persimmon tree
Is clear as a wineglass stem.

In *Paradiso*
A river of hosts
Opens to the poet
Who begs and prays
For an illumined soul.
And I saw light
That took a river's form —
Light flashing,
Reddish-gold,
Between two banks
Painted with wonderful
Spring flowerings....

Finger reading,
A tempered exercise,
I notice how dark
The window has become
Though it's noon
And August

And daylight still resists winter.
I bow my head,
Return to the book.

Poor poet,
He hurries to the river,
And *into* the river,
His eyes as wide
As a man can make them.
The long sunlight of late summer
Floods the rhododendrons —
This is the light
That pulls him
Under the stream,
Hands, lips, fingers, opening...

The river
And the gems
Of topaz
Entering and leaving,
And the grasses' laughter —
These are shadows,
Prefaces of their truth....

I strain for color,
The preclusion of sight,
And put aside the book,
Paradiso in braille.

Who the hell is this
Turning again to the window,
His fingers reaching the sill,
Hands still touching
A river that no one can see?

Serenade

What can I tell you
Except that birds
Came to me that summer
As if I were St. Jerome
Instead of the crippled kid
Who spent his time alone.

I was a muddy rat.
I spoke across the water.
I moved with my hands.

Blackbirds whistled
Through the dry creek bed.
The cemetery called the purple martins.

The boy I speak of
Went from fence to stone
Very like a bird —
And like a bird
He would listen
In the tall grass.

When the birds came
He rose through the tatter of clouds.
The boy with two faces, he flew through clouds.
The kid who couldn't see, he flew right up.
His parents came, they banged on pots and pans;
They hoped to get him back to earth.

But they were far below,
And the boy was in the sky of verities.

The child had passed away,
Had arrived at a kind of end,
A bird place,
Where life hangs on a spin.

You can live in matchless grace.

At the Woods' Edge

As I get older
The incidental lyric
Slips through the dark trees,
But honestly I can't tell
What it means—

I build a fire
With the split sections of a birch
That leaned in former times
Above the standing water
Of a neighbor's pond,

And I turn back to the table.
A Little Thing,
The Quantity of an Hazel Nut—
The homeliness of God,
Julian of Norwich.

That good woman
Lifted a nut,
Visioned the Lord,
Was swept by the all-thing,
As round as a ball
In the palm of her hand.

In the arbor
Birch and hazel are related,
Though distantly.

I picture Julian
Walking in the kindly light,
Picking up her filberts.

They must have shone,
Excremental and gold
In the morning dew.

In the Americas
We have the witch hazel
And the assorted birches,
None of which produce
A facsimile of the homely
And edible
Nuts of Norwich.

Now and then
The fire grabs hold
Of a birch twig.
It sounds
As if someone's
Whistling.

Diagram

By chance I'll grow
My own persimmon tree
With its odd and even clusters
Of hanging seeds.
This is the job
Of sentient beings,
The tacit construction
Of organic neurology —
What they used to call the self.
It opens, midday
In Italian sun
Or the botanic gardens
Of Brooklyn.
It spreads
All night
Without stars,
A seine net,
Albino branches...

Guiding Eyes

Corky, a yellow Labrador

It's been five years
Since I was paired with this dog
Who, in fact, is more than a dog —
She watches for me.

Our twin minds go walking,
And I suspect as we enter the subway
On Lexington
That we're a kind of centaur —
Or maybe two owls
Riding the shoulders of Minerva.
The traffic squalls and plunges
At Columbus Circle,
Seethes down Broadway,
And we step out
Into the blackness
That alarmed Pascal:
The emptiness
Between stars.

I suppose we're scarcely whole
If I think on it —
We walk on a dead branch,
Two moths still attached,
The inert day poised above us,
The walls of the canyon looming.

Did I think on it?

A blessing opens by degrees
And I must walk
Both bodily and ghostly
Down Fifth Avenue,
Increasing my devotion full much
To the postulate of arrival —
To how I love this inexhaustible dog
Who leads me
Past jackhammers
And the police barriers
Of New York.

All day snow falls
On the disorderly crowds,
It clothes Miss Corky
Until her tawny fur
Carries the milky dirt
Of ocean and stone.

The centaur gathers
What passes from our flesh
Into the heart
Of animal faith.

Meanwhile
She guides me home.

Only Bread, Only Light

At times the blind see light,
And that moment is the Sistine ceiling,

Grace among buildings — no one asks
For it, no one asks.

After all, this is solitude,
Daylight's finger,

Blake's angel
Parting willow leaves.

I should know better.
Get with the business

Of walking the lovely, satisfied,
Indifferent weather —

Bread baking
On Arthur Avenue

This first warm day of June.
I stand on the corner

For priceless seconds.
Now everything to me falls shadow.

Two

Still

The old love seeps
Like pond water
In your shoes,
And the field is bracken
Under snow.
Who loves you, who doesn't:
Each curls like burning paper
And blooms upward
In the winter dusk.
Orion spins.

The old love begins
To waltz you
Across the yard
Until you sway.
Who loves you, who doesn't:
Each tastes like iron,
But new love
Was never a nail
And tastes of snow.

At the pond's edge
You test new ice
By tossing old ice
And listening.

Drink

Helsinki, Mannerheim Street

The glory of chance
And the hazard of death
Met each other
On a windy street —

Two rainshadows,
Brothers
With the papery, blue faces
Of old money,

Their cloaks
Like palpitant wings,
Angels of riot
Under winter poplars.

They saw, each to each,
The dark-tongued
And unthreaded
Pigments of philos,

Knowing how indecorous it was,
Love, shining like that
In the other's face —
While somewhere in the trees

The crows went fighting
Over a starling's eye.
Two kinsmen in rain,
Rain to snow.

Post-Orphic

Tonight I felt it in my ribs:
A flood of green in the marrow,

And I decided to live right here
And sing sometimes.

I pulled a book from its shelf,
Held the minutiae of the world

Open like a killdeer's wings.
I've lived without names

For plants and trees.
What happens now?

What happens?

Summary at North Farm

Finnish rural life, ca. 1910

Fires, always fires after midnight,
The sun depending in the purple birches

And gleaming like a copper kettle.
By the solstice they'd burned everything,

The bad-luck sleigh, a twisted rocker,
Things "possessed" and not quite right.

The bonfire coils and lurches,
Big as a house, and then it settles.

The dancers come, dressed like rainbows
(If rainbows could be spun),

And linking hands they turn
To the melancholy fiddles.

A red bird spreads its wings now
And in the darker days to come.

Helsinki, 1958

Exiled Russians lingered over tea
As the skylights

Turned the harbor mist
To bands of color:

Streaks of blue on damask,
Shifting yellows,

And then crimson
On their bloodless faces

And silvered hair.
They wore ermine capes,

Heavy crosses,
And shared a smoker's squint

Acknowledging
Chess moves.

None of them
Thought to write a book

About the flight
Across frozen lakes

Or the dead
Who look for us

During our lives.
They went on drinking tea

Without ambition —
Like men who remain

Where their houses once stood.

Facing the Trees

after the Finnish of Risto Rasa

1

We turn to the woods:
They stand
Like a gate,

A green door
Half-open
Giving light.

By midsummer
Guests will come,
But now

Birches
Fill
With a kingdom

Of birds.

2

In the morning
After a night of rain
We move slowly

Gathering memories
By the lake —

The scent
Of soaked earth
Like a good dream.

We say
Sweet rain
Frees the mushrooms.

Our lives
Whirl
Around us

Like winged seeds.
Nightfall
Junipers

Stand lost
Between earth and sky.

3

Moonbeams
Open gold eyes
In the stones.

The dog comes home
After dark.
As he circles

And falls asleep,
His warmth of heart
Spreads through every room.

for Juhani Lindholm

In the Attic

The radio vibrates imperceptibly;
I'd forgotten it was on
And turn the volume up—but slowly.
Bach: "Invention no. 13"...
Then the involuntary shiver!
Glenn Gould! Hailstones
Through the skylights!

for Anselm Hollo

Praise for the Yiddish Poets

It should be easy to carry the morning on our backs,
The sky weighs less at sunup, but you knew that.
And you knew how the long march
With the heavy wagon... how that story
Became the children — it's in the milk,
A tin-pail taste before the words began.
You take up a pencil and write:
I've lived in so many towns;
Everywhere, the milk turns
Before it reaches the table.
Then, modestly, you cross out the towns,
Cross out the table, *everywhere*
Is replaced by the morning star.
Milk tastes less of tin,
More of *odori*, wild herbs
Growing beside the road.

Lying Still

It's a dog's life, so his life curls
In a doggy circle: he sits in himself that way,
Occupied by density, uncatchable by speed.
It's just before eating when the wind sways him
That he feels the itch of people,
A hammering from the misbegotten.
We have to choose between the wild in us
And the sober, between the painter
And the stamp collector —
He talks to himself like a surgeon
And clicks his spoon.
Inside his skull a tent
Falls on everything:
The cottage where he fished
And the boat that carried him,
The buttons on Margaret's blouse.
When dumb, he thinks, we lived at our highest.
The slow harmony of his house
Is a doggy fantasia, the unboxed truth,
And the unexpected stars come out,
Fat and imperfect.
He turns in a circle
Surveying live hopes
And dead ones.
He accepts stillness
But feels tricked by time:
Yesterday was absolute, clear,
Filled with turns,

And he raises his spoon
At one remove from the weather—

Ubi sunt? he thinks, like any dog,
Where are they now?

Competing Interests within the Family: 1909

My mother's father built motorcars.
They weren't loud enough, so he built motorcycles.
They weren't fast enough; he produced dynamite.
The dynamite wasn't far enough — he made mortar shells.
By then it was November and Johanna Gadski
Was appearing in *Aida* opposite Caruso.
My mother's mother bought the record
(Victor Matrix C-8348-2).
In general it is believed that people who make puns
Suffer from contradictory impulses.
My grandmother never made puns.
"Victrola" is a neologism; it replaces nothing.
And what if all of animate nature
Be but organic harps diversely framed
That tremble into thought?
The record plays; windows rattle.

At the Summer House

A curtain falls in the midday heat.
Boats swing around at their moorings.

The rain pours first along the shore,
Then advances on a stand of pines

Where it hisses in dry needles.
Lightning circles the lake all afternoon.

I move through the house
Wanting to be carried like a child

Who needs to see all the rooms
Before he sleeps. And faces

Recollected — stars
On the retinas —

Shimmer as though I'd rubbed my eyes —
My grandfather rowing on a still day,

His young wife with a broad-brimmed hat.
These are bright now,

And then gone, like minnows
Darting in the shallows.

First Things

At dawn, standing, first things.
Orchids, if you're lucky.
Do you believe in luck?
Some friends do.
Some whisper to their houses.

I'm prayerful, first light...
No hymn... a brief thing,
Sun on water...
Some will say the world *worlds,*
Some will whisper.

A blue heron startles Ross,
Age ten, up early for the fish.
We find out. Luck is a verb;
To walk, a noun...
The first sun through the trees

Is a chord of light, sun
Is music, adagio cantabile.
Do I believe in luck?
I believe we close our eyes.
The boy laughs. Sound of wings.

Waiting

Is part of something: a blue door opens,
Portuguese fishermen walk from a coffee shop

In Providence, Rhode Island — or Lisbon —
And head for the pier with buckets.

Part of something, they ride the sea:
The Atlantic, part of something.

Mornings on the coast, houses
In fog on the hills, the paint

Like carnival pastels… People believe
The whole world is part of something.

The phone rings… they give it away.
I spoke last night with a friend… He might

One day become your friend, or sometime,
Far off, a friend to your children —

Part of something. I told him
About the English poet

Who, deserting God, still loved
With clean irony the churches

On country roads… He'd lean his bike
And go inside — not certain of motive

But to wait, because others had waited
In just that place, sitting through the sunset

Beneath the slender windows.

Three

Deus Faber

Plenty is no dainty, the English say.
Let's pretend we're eating, the title
Of a Finnish folktale.

Wisdom differs
According to calories.
The longer by the fire

The sooner he feels the cold.
Last night new frost
Swept over the lawns,

Freezing the brown-gilled
Mushrooms — the Lawn Mower's
Delight, *Psathyrella foenisecii* —

Edible, parchment umbrellas
Scattered in the icy grass.
Like most Finns

I flatter myself,
Pretend to mushroom savvy.
Skins moist with hanging veils,

The slightly fibrous
Cinnamon-brown caps
Of the Saffron Cort —

It remains in late fall
While others fold.
They resemble Russian domes,

Toy churches
That arrived in the garden
While the neighbors slept

And the houses
Began a winter's feed
On oil and coal.

In Finland, in Karstula,
Ur-village of my father,
They ate salted roots,

Black parsnips,
Cloudberries,
Wormwood,

Päivällispöytään —
Daily to the table...
In birch groves

The fairy rings
Of yellow-to-orange
Cottony, sweet fungi

Stood, stone-still,
Enchanted
In ice,

Their hats bruised red...
And so a joy
The mushroom then,

Buttery snail,
Chiffon finger,
Dainty of marshland.

The cookbooks
Of old Suomi
Penetrate the heavy frost —

When hungry,
Never search for mushrooms,
Look-alikes may fool you then.

When famished, cook with great care.

Tourists

One night in London
My wife and I visited 221B
Baker Street, fictional home
To Sherlock Holmes,
A restaurant in fact.

We ate in the shadows
Of a Victorian parlor
Decked with velvet drapes,
Maroon, I think.
There was plenty of tough meat
And the obligatory cheese
Had a gamy taste.

Our table stood by a door
That opened on the winter street —
A tin bell chimed like mad
As the Conan-Doyle-ists
Filed in — an oddly drunken lot,
An Eastern fraternal order,
Poles or Hungarians,
Anyway, men wearing fezzes.

All were ushered
By a silent girl
Clothed as a scullery maid.
They drank toasts
To the genius of Mr. Holmes

And trooped up rickety stairs
To view his reputed apartments,
A cluster of tiny rooms
Where assorted poisons
Were displayed —

Row after row
Of leaded bottles
With associated charts
Outlining the tendons
And chief arteries
Of the human body.
What a dish, toxicology.

Alongside the Masons of Kraków
We signed the guest book
And escaped to our hotel
Where later, deep at night,
We woke, sweating
As if someone had slipped us
Amanita muscaria,

A mushroom only mildly toxic,
Though it causes, invariably,
Stupefaction,
As if you'd been dining
With the brotherhood sinister.

Sheraton, Chicago, Three A.M.

Dreams stretch out
A wilderness before us,
The hills empty of trees,

Sunset pouring fast
Through the high passes.
I met a man there

Who, as Yeats would say,
"Was no right man."
The western sky

Lay behind him,
His face was lost
In the pointed sun —

A corridor from Hades.
"I thought you were my brother,"
He said, looking me over,

"But you are still alive
And only dream
Like one of us…"

Then the sun was gone
And the unfamiliar bed
Closed around me.

The tenor of a room,
Worlds without dimension,
The ambient furnishings.

Among a million living souls
I move through space
With hands outstretched.

My brother, I think,
Lives, climbing the steep
Of a ravine — here

Where two of us,
High above Lake Michigan,
Stir the composite sugars

In a cup of first light.

In Our Time

Who knows?
I lie down on my side
As though it's a necessary game,
Hearing the war drums,
Checking the corollary birds
That betray the movements
Of spies…

I'm hidden
By the toothed, simple leaves
Of the English holly — an evergreen,
It conceals us
From public tragedies,
Has concealed us.

Over the brim of trouble
Poetry continues,
The yellow poplar
Does its damnedest
To hold me.
The alder
Drops red-to-purple
And consecrated strings
At the cemetery's edge.

Who believes
In the sublime infancies
And virgin apprehensions

Of children
Among the sweet birches?

I remain motionless
Like Thomas Traherne
And listen for the bees
From the estate of innocence.

In the thick shade
The maple seeds
Rise like sparks
Just out of reach.

I speak for the boy
Who, before all others,
Played our game.

He played it while collecting twigs.
He lay stock-still on the earth
And listened to the Orient wind.

The trees are foreign soldiers
Talking low in a different tongue.

Mandelstam

The age, the beast came home tonight,
The oak leaves torn in holy disorder.

There was a wheel, a rolling fire;
There was a street;

It swelled with bronze and sadness.
I can be trusted: here are the crumbs

Of my earth and freedom.

Tenth Muse

By now I should be used to this,
This looking to the tops of trees
And seeing nothing —
No pearl-jade curtains,
Not a single nest.

Blindness is a long, inlet wave —
Even at noon the swimmers vanish
As when Odysseus saw ghosts,
Distinguished them from weeds
Or stones... and they were gone.

Here is the shore.
This season of cataract,
Even the shallows, true emerald,
Promise some erotic terror.

The Approximate Hour

Rain took the mountains late in the day —
A reprieve, as if we'd danced the proper steps
With the goats. Rain from Ontario,

September turning out its pockets,
A tin dish overflowing on a stone.
The Adirondacks were formal,

Raising votive cups.

for Deborah Tall and David Weiss

Allegro

Because I'm astonished by your
Astonishment at me, that is,

The Essene *idea* of me, this
Evangelical man before you —

Because of this I take up the piano
And playing by ear, I think

How empty the fields...
Music, even poorly conceived

Music, astounds you, as it should,
Our saying in the high-hearted darkness,

Lights off with December's candles,
Let us warm ourselves

With Mister Fats Waller.
And I play "Ain't Misbehavin'"

And you astonish me,
Knowing every word.

Prism

Just as water breaks
Through fallen branches,
Sunlight darts like needlefish
Enduring the bonds
Of H_2 and O.
Surely there's a cause
Behind the impulse:
The angstrom
With its Viennese angels
Spins — and time, the poor cousin,
Pushes clouds.

2

Light sweeps grains of sand,
Heats the ferrous oxide —
Water becomes gracious
And lifts the warmer oxygens.
The sardines rise.
My friend Kalevi Makkonen
Pulls his nets
And there it is,
A wave of tossing light
Brought up from the sea.
The precision

Of happiness
Remains a mystery.

3

Boats return to harbor
In the Åland Islands.
The sun drops swiftly
Behind the fishermen's church.
Toasts are made
And light divides
At the rim of a glass.
A persistence
Without tears.
And again
Light streams
Through the odd angles
Of dishes
And lifted hands.

Knossos

All afternoon I climbed
Following a country girl
And an old man... surely
It was possible in their company
That the mythic lives of climbers
Would reach me, or in fact
Possess me — the validity
Of Greek story
Said it was so.
I believed it, spun in air,
Pulled at vines.
The old man had climbed so fast
I guessed he was *Paraklētos,*
The weird Holy Ghost
Who lives with certainty
In every village
On the island of Crete.
So the man was a god.
The girl — his granddaughter?
She was his equal.
And the high, solar heart
Of limestone
Pulsed for them
As it does
For its own,
Until, I have to say,
Apart, and with humility,
They went evenly
Into the sun.

The Invention of the Wolf

Literature was not born on the day
A boy crying "Wolf, Wolf,"
Came running out of the Neanderthal valley
With a big gray wolf at his heels:
Literature was born on the day
When a boy came crying "Wolf, Wolf,"
And there was no wolf behind him.

VLADIMIR NABOKOV

It's certain: the boy came crying
And there was no wolf,
There were only the loblolly pines,
The shingle oaks, the ailanthus,
The staghorn sumac —
In short, a forest, and be assured
It *was* a forest for the trees
Were at least thirteen feet high,
Which is, I'm told, the height at which
Trees are trees and not just shrubs —
But there was no wolf, no wolf at all.
There were birds: the cassowary,
The dodo, the apocolocytos,
That bird with the radiant entrails
Which, when stretched across a baking stone,
Turned in a wink from purplish-red to yellow
And thereby told you tons
About the life expectancy
Of the unmitigated tribe,
But there was no wolf, no wolf at all.
The ropy grass was full of fireflies,
The electric flies

Of the Neanderthal valley
That shone like spotlights
Over the boy's face
As he spoke in the lip-stretched patois
Of the Indus, clicking his root-stained teeth.
O flow on... no wolf spelled backward
First narrative trick,
First trickster —
Of mind, of capacity,
Nature then, then feeling,
No wolf, no wolf...
And true wolves quivered in their sleep.

Open Window

When leaves are shaken, dry rustle
Of gardens, dogs maybe,
I stop to hear the lingua of old hunger.

Atlas steals the apples of Hesperides,
Runs to the tall grass
Where he gorges unobserved.

Who would say that appetite
Is not of the ear?
I lean at the window

In the high peak of my house
And the concentric sounds:
Birds, children, doors,

Each rouses a craving,
The vatic hint of things
Proving to our thinnest bones

The human wish
For candied flowers, cold milk,
Black bread.

Atlas?
His apples are a yellow-gold
Still unseen.

Wind. Salt grass.
A screen door clatters.
More hunger there.

King of the Crickets

The little boy went looking for his voice.
The King of the crickets had it.

FEDERICO GARCÍA LORCA

The boy was forgotten... weeds grew.
The poem was filed away, a dead letter

In New York, town of arsenic lobsters...
I don't know — the boy, that voice,

The King of the crickets,
They live in the Etruscan lungs.

I might as well discuss the history
Of the human wrist, or the Greek word *skandalon,*

Which appears in Revelation
And can't be translated.

A cricket spirals through the grass.
A boy looks everywhere.

He hears wind in the wild roses.
Who has time to breathe?

Summary: Boys and crickets
Sing with their legs. The theft,

The pursuit, one and the same.
The Greek word *doxa* means

Both "opinion" and "glory."
The little boy went looking for his voice.

Crickets glorify the wheat.
Who has time to think?

Breton-esque

poets in their youth

We stopped beside the road,
Two bantering monks
In the wild-carrot leaf,
Each dimmed by acquired reading
And reposing now in the verdure
Of persons gently unhappy.

Our saints were nothing but rhythms:
J'ai brassé mon sang, I said,
I have brewed my blood.
I swore St. Francis was Rimbaud,
That we were consecrated to anxiety
And we'd be dangerous by and by.

Exotic with immanence,
We recited from Nerval,
Then Mallarmé,
Whose poverty you loved.
Paltry friend,
What atrocious vigils we owed!

The bats came out
To poems of execrable love.
I read Lorca like a menu
As we dropped to our knees —
Rare connoisseurs —
And chewed the cemetery grass.

Rachmaninoff's Curtains

All it takes is the fading light
And the human condition talks
But firmly, in a juristic way:

Weak sun, we round our mouths;
It can't be helped —
We confide in the police

As if we were children
Lost in neighborhoods
Almost ours.

The maestro, hearing
He was dying,
Took a Brahman voyage

Up the stairs,
Entered his study,
Closed the door,

And with curtains drawn
Spoke slowly to his hands.
His tongue was so much heavier

Than those brown and gold instruments
There in the kindly dusk
Of receiving keys.

Running to the Wood

My dog, trained for the blind,
Sees Rorschachs of wings.
Vows of light, tongueless stones
Call her to the door.

All gods are avatars of width.
They dance a bone dance
Down the centuries of June.
Dispensed by mists, I'm lonely too.

The Roman gravity of our lives is inconsolable.

Viaticum

1

The Tao of walking, say, the American roadside,
Though it won't be leisure brings you out.

It's money that walks us through the beach grass.
There are broken devices here...

2

When he was a boy
My father shoveled railway tracks.

Later he called it *misery mud* —
A good word in Finnish.

The funny thing was, he'd say,
I used to shovel up people's teeth.

And I mean regularly.

Essay on November

There is at times a small fire
In the brain, partita for violin,
Brier, black stem,
All burning in the quarter notes.
And the hedgerow
Beyond the barn
Calls its starlings in.
Then frost, sere leaves,
A swollen half-moon
Like a drowsy fingertip
Above the apple trees.

Mnemosyne

A drugstore in Helsinki... glass bottles at the window...
snow from another century falling... One pictures the czar's
nurse arriving by sleigh... her search for laudanum... the
empress with a toothache. Thank God for chemists in
provincial towns!

Why does the goddess favor a drugstore?

The postulate of memory and sickness... between sheets...
between fevers and night sweat... glass bottles arranged
like a bedside choir... bottles arrayed like pieces in a game
of chess...

Peruvian rhatany — opens the throat...

Achene — ripe ovaries of roses... fertility powder...

Verbena — crushed petals, Anglo-Saxon cure-all...

The bottles pass around the world.

It's midnight in an arctic city.

A single light and the vials burning like memory's candles.

"Revolution by Night"

Whenever I'm awake at 4 A.M., I call Max Ernst. He keeps
rooms in three far-off cities: Muonio (Lapland), Cooch Behar
(Bengal), and Tirlemont (Belgium).

Why do I bother with Max?

Before he died he buried a prestamped passport.

Credentials to a world without borders.

It's nothing more than a broken fan.

Stamped between the folds it says: *There are no more
real birds.*

Hold it against the light, there's an essay on
"Indifferentism."

It says all things are a matter of indifference except virtue,
which is the only thing that has intrinsic worth.

(I don't know about you, but I side with Adelard of Bath:
ideas are particular or universal according to the point of
view from which they are regarded.)

Consider the broken fan.

Tilt it and the words disappear.

(The asociological imperative of light!)

Even the sentence on virtue is impossible to read!

"The Indigo Bird is a real bird."

(I'm speaking aloud.)

(It's four A.M. and I'm talking out loud in room 1027 of the Millennium Hotel on 42nd Street in New York.)

I talk as if I'm on the phone.

It's warm on the tenth floor.

I fan Max's passport under my nose.

Descant on Climbing and Descending Stairs

1

In the summer of 1959 I discovered my first Victrola while exploring the attic of my grandparents' house. That house was a sprawling Victorian temple: tunnels and dusty stairs led a boy up five flights to stand at last in a cupola of light. If you listened you could hear bees under the sagging floor.

I was listening. My job was to keep track of sounds. Maybe this had to do with my failing eyesight. Maybe not. I was slipping down the throat of life. I was caught trying to hear the viscera of things.

No one can explain the sharpness of certain sounds.

There's a music that comes in the curious places where we stop to rest.

I remember some moments perfectly.

The bees like a millstone turning under the oak boards.

Wasps striking glass like thrown buttons.

The intervals of silence, harsh as waves in the past or future.

The inflorescence of spiderwebs and soot.

A yellow afternoon in high summer.

And the Victrola in the arched gateway of endless time.
I approached the abandoned machine like a naked
fisherman.

2

Even a boy understands that "Victrola" is a neologism — the
device arrives one day without warning like a suit of armor
with a human being inside. There's never been a thing
like it!

It stood on a table, the horn imperial. I drew as close as I
dared — within a foot — then waited to be certain that it
wouldn't move.

When I was satisfied, I reached out and touched it.

At once the platter turned and there was a groan!

The long needle was still perched in the groove of a disc.

I spun the record with my index finger and produced a
pitiless, unformed sound, a wrought-iron hinge, or the noise
of blood in the body's memory.

Spinning again I heard the raging wind from some
unidentifiable continent.

I pictured the neck of the horn, that black maw, holding
men, faces, eyes, and opened hands.

Sarcophagus of souls and smoke...

I remained in the cupola until sunset, turning the record to
and fro.

3

Sound, like love, can be sudden and threatening.

I had to return to the Victrola several times before I
understood its mechanism.

I climbed the forgotten stairs and found that by turning the
handle you could set the record spinning freely.

The recording was Caruso's "Vesti la giubba."

Canio, the clown and murderer... the hollow needle...
a noise of pitching metal and wax... a "live" sound that
seemed to cross a great distance... as if a vital man was
singing through a steam pipe from a room in a cellar.

Then the frightful laughter... I ran each time I heard it...
the cachinnation of a madman suddenly rising from the
enormous bell of the trumpet...

I returned to the attic a dozen times that summer before I
finally heard the aria in full.

The Victrola sang from its great, crackling heart.

And my own heart raced, both running and returning.

The Sleep I Didn't Sleep

Is slept by another man
Who finds a place in the trees

And watches the middle distance,
Liking a fool's work.

He takes time with nonsense:
The obvious fortune

Of the ego — that clean nowhere.
He makes sleep flicker like a rail

And dreams a persimmon tree,
A surge of starlings in a hedge,

A pond black as a fig,
And the night drapes him

In grainy sweetness
Until he feels easy

And transient.
It doesn't matter

Who loves him, who doesn't.
He sees the rain, undiminished

Behind his every thought.

"Talking Books"

I can still hear that actor's voice
With its bass notes, or the static
And hiss of records played all afternoon.

They'd arrive in black, metallic cartons,
Their labels faded, *Matter for the Blind,*
Or *Library of Congress.*

I'd follow each rhapsodic
Twist — Peary tries to find
The path through emptiness,

Crossing polar ice —
Or Huck slips away
From the Widow's fetters,

And the needle would stick — then silence.
I'd flip it over,
Feeling for the center

With practiced fingers,
As the Duke and Dauphin hovered
In blackness all the while,

Suspended in their violence.
Books might last for days,
But I had them to afford

In half-light, and dark ascensions,
Listening without moving.
The machine was Government Issue,

A veteran of the New Deal
(The blind began to "read" in that depression —)
It sent off heat like a stove.

I leaned close, clutching a tissue,
And heard the reader's stern appeal:
This book resumes on the next record...

Elegy for Ted Berrigan

When I heard you read, I was only twenty,
But I knew you were a fool.
It was your weakened vanity
That did it — none of the "cool"

Poets in my required reading
Ever filled their work
With Pepsi or fucking
Or the weather in New York.

Neruda made a science of tears,
Yeats had his vision.
Roethke danced from ear to ear,
While Rilke served a mission.

Their poems were philosophy:
A rage for "God" or order
Lurked in each apostrophe.
Poetry was "harder" —

A crystal, the center
Of static divination.
By reading, one could enter
The drama of creation.

You were vulnerability —
It was gloomy being broke today;

I am in love with poetry;
Love, why do you always take my heart away?

I didn't know then
That there'd be days like this —
Weeks… months when
Making an honest list

Is all that finally matters.
(There's no art in being real;
Who can change it later?)
At twenty, I was pure dismissal.

I didn't want to hear
Your frail, lovely voice
Reciting pills and fear.
I thought you'd made a choice;

I thought that poets had command
Of verse — I praised conviction
And luck. I thought I had a hand
In my own destination.

Ode to Ogden Nash

later, he was mean…

Okay Nash, it's early spring
And I just broke a ten-cent thing,

Shall I give you an account?
Should you know (and here

I see you dressed in pajamas,
No longer funny, severely alone) —

Should you know what a comic I am?
Or that tonight I walked to a church

To sit with the neighborhood drunks
And the tears swelled us,

Seven men, like wooden boats?
Well who knows?

Mister Nash, it's April
And I know how your spirit went:

Laughter ended up in languishment.
We make our planetary beds.

I talk out loud
Like one who piles stones.

Who can be equal to talk?
It's the middle of the sweating night

And what good does it do to know
That the light in every shadow

Is the shadow?

Ode to My Sleeping Pills

Dusk that passes
Through a priest's glove,
Evening with spring birds,
It's good of you to wait
Like the sister
Who gives out bread
At the convent —
Where even late
A line of children
Stands at the window,
The bread a dry whisper
From her invisible hands.

Each warm bundle
Includes its black feather,
Sticks from the first nest.
With these you comb my hair,
Smooth my face,
Perfect me in secret
Like the rose
That was eaten at dawn
By that early pope
Whose name I won't remember.

The Mockingbird on Central

This bird who lands in the oak tree
Is both a comedian *and* a natural fact:

In a hundred-years house
We awaken to a sweet thing,

A motor of avian laughter
Ten feet from our curtain.

This is fortune. He sings "La Paloma,"
"Wiener Bonbons,"

L'heure exquise,
Noel Coward, *Tonight at 8:30.*

What precocity, a bird half the size
Of an Anjou pear

Who flirts like Galli-Curci,
Shows off like Caruso,

And all from an oak branch
Swaying above our porch.

O how he brags at three A.M.!
O how he imitates the happiness of others!

for Connie

Corazón, Corazón

I asked of every heart
If it held
Something more —
Something almost weightless
Like those nearly invisible fish in Lapland
That you'd swear
Are about to grow feathers
And fly.

Of course
I spoke the heart's language
Like a foreigner,
Contending
With the metallic taste
Of unfamiliar vowels,
And of course
My mistakes
Were tragicomic —

For *love* I said *wheel of fire;*
For *gratitude, dense blue air;*
My sibilants confused
So that speaking of perfume
I said *blubber in gobbets.*
Let me tell you
I was an immigrant,
And in fact, many hearts
Thought I was a moron!

How unfair this was!
All I wanted was a metaphysical conversation
About George Herbert's flowers —
If the poet grew a garland
And shared it with his girl
And with God,
Which flowers would those have been?
But as you can imagine
Instead of *garland*
I said *garlic* —
And more than once,
So that my reputation as an imbecile
Was well established
In the sub-rosa world of heartspeak.

Nothing is more intolerant
Than the native heart
Forced to engage
Recondite chatterboxes
Babbling pure Berlitz —
To such hearts
The ordinary mortal sounds
Like a warped phonograph record.

Sometimes though,
Two hearts meet
Much as those invisible fish

Of Lapland
Swooshing against each other
In the lightless lakes.
It happens at first without a word,
Hearts depending together
In the rust and grass
Of their mythic places.

And you know
Hearts can get lucky —
Those people attached
Might not say *garlic*
Until their second date,
And we all know
Garlic is good for the heart,
Even though
It was hoping
You'd say *laurel*
Or *bay leaf*.

This poem is for those who say *garlic*
And get married anyway.

for Kurt Kuss and Barbara Ceconi

Four

Seven Prayers

the loss of reading vision

Prime

In the deep, dread summer heat
I lie on the floor of a borrowed cabin,
And with incense and meadow silence
The scapular music of the green
And submissive man
Stirs a counterwish.
How else to say the body's grief
Speaks in every particular?
Beyond the screens
In tall cinnamon ferns
The baby crows are fighting,
Their ready flesh
Instant as fire.
The cobwebbed muscles
Behind my eyes
Have been burning for a week.
It's been months since I've read a book.

Terce

This morning I asked for the opening
Of my body's gates, that sunlight
Would touch the bones of my face.
We wait for our lives
And the equivocal judgments of light.

The monarch butterflies
Climb the silver birch
Just beyond my door.

Sext

Walls of the city are built,
Your shadow stretches away from harm.
See Aristotle, standing in a tidal pool,
Counting on his fingers.
He'll outlast unmerited suffering.

You of course must take your own sweet way,
Puzzle in the limestone,
Move the wall, rock by rock,
Find the stone that fits your back.

It's the rapture of looking
That gives us want.
The bearberries have ripened.

The veins of a leaf
Are the Paleocene acrostic,
A blended flesh, almost occult.

Nones

I ate of the shadow, the shadow
Ate of me. The scouring bees of blindness
Merge with the wood of self
Until even my face in water
Is past memory.
                    Left alone with my day —
Attending to whatever bird,
I breathe
As if I might be anyone
With the peasant freedom
To guess at everything.
Supposing a place to live
Is what the eyes do.
Bird, street, house.

Vespers

The lacerating tune of the house
Is the song we never finish:
Even the queen talked aloud
To her dead husband
And spread before him
The day's occasional pictures.
Unexpected fireflies appear
Along a hedgerow —
We stand in the open door
Taking the lower way,
Pronouncing each word
For our private, qualified dead.

Compline

Moon of nuance, moon of vanity,
Your meridian names
Were known by the blind
In Brueghel's painting.

What creatured image climbs your trellis?

Laud

I'll let the birch tree stand
For the closed purchase
Of the outer world...

Warm my name, entreat me,
Summon new faces from the grass
That the barest chance will seem a wedding,
That the sealed routes of growing will be lined
With well-wishers.

Birch tree, is it true
Our every breath is a wish
Whether we will it or not —
Each cuneiform spasm
A message?

Silver birch with your three trunks,
I'm coming out
To walk the trees.

Night Seasons

Up late, reading alone,
I feed printed pages
Into the Kurzweil scanner,
An electronic reader
For the blind.

Randomly now
I take books from my shelves,
Open the mysterious volumes,
And lay them flat on the machine.
I can't say
What's coming next —
I wait in perfect silence
For the voice to begin,
This synthetic child
Reading to an old man.

The body, stalled,
Picks fragments,
Frottage,
Scraps of paper,
Whatever comes.

Pico della Mirandola,
Egyptian love poems,
Essene communes beside the Red Sea,
Paavo Haavikko's "König Harald"…

An old professor,
Bitter at the graceful way
The poets have
Of gathering terms
Inexactly,
Told me, "The poets are fools.
They read
Only in fragments."

I'm the fool
Of the night seasons,
Reading anything, *anything*.
When daylight comes
And you see me on the street
Or standing for the bus,
Think of the Greek term
Entelechy,
Word for soul and body
Constructing each other
After dark.

About the Author

Stephen Kuusisto was born in 1955 in Exeter, New Hampshire and grew up in Helsinki, Finland; coastal New England; and western New York. He is a graduate of the Writers' Workshop at the University of Iowa. He has taught at the University of Iowa, Hobart and William Smith Colleges, and now teaches in the graduate writing program at Ohio State University in Columbus, Ohio. His memoir, *Planet of the Blind*, was named a "Notable Book of the Year" by *The New York Times*. His essays and poems have appeared in numerous magazines, including *Harper's, The New York Times Magazine, Poetry,* and *Seneca Review*.

The Chinese character for poetry (*shih*) combines "word" and "temple." It
also serves as pressmark and raison d'être for Copper Canyon Press.
Founded in 1972, Copper Canyon Press remains dedicated to publishing
poetry exclusively, from Nobel laureates to new and emerging authors.
The Press thrives with the generous patronage of readers, writers,
booksellers, librarians, teachers, and students — everyone who shares
the conviction that poetry clarifies and deepens social and
spiritual awareness. We invite you to join
this community of supporters.

FOUNDER'S CIRCLE

Allen Foundation for the Arts
Jaech Family Foundation
Lannan Foundation
Lila Wallace–Reader's Digest Fund
National Endowment for the Arts
Washington State Arts Commission

PUBLISHER'S CIRCLE

Leslie and Janet Cox
Cynthia Hartwig
Rhoady and Jeanne Marie Lee
Emily Warn
Witter Bynner Foundation for Poetry

READER'S CIRCLE

Thatcher Bailey
Gregory Baran and Laura Federighi
Hugh and Jane Ferguson Foundation
Mimi Gardner Gates
Bill and Sammy Greenwood
Gull Industries
Laura Ingham
Bruce S. Kahn
Alida and Christopher Latham
Peter Lewis, Campagne
William and Kristine O'Daly
Karen Swenson
Jim and Mary Lou Wickwire
Wyman Youth Trust

For information and catalogs:
COPPER CANYON PRESS
Post Office Box 271
Port Townsend, Washington 98368
360/385-4925 • poetry@coppercanyonpress.org
www.coppercanyonpress.org

This book is set in the digital version of Figural,
designed by Oldřich Menhart in 1940, and
redrawn for Letraset in 1992 by Michael Gills.
Book design by Valerie Brewster, Scribe Typography.
Printed on archival-quality Glatfelter Author's Text
by McNaughton & Gunn, Inc.